VOLUME 2

The Butterfly
SHADING
A Grayscale Coloring Book

COLORING BOOK FOR ADULTS

COLOR TEST PAGE

www.ingramcontent.com/pod-product-compliance
Lightning Source LLC
Chambersburg PA
CBHW052014280526
45793CB00005B/979

* 9 7 8 1 5 3 5 3 0 1 8 9 3 *